Table of Contents

Introduction

The bladder is a hollow, flexible pouch in your pelvis. Its main job is to store urine before it leaves your body. Your kidneys make pee. Tubes called ureters carry the pee from your kidneys to your bladder. When you use the bathroom, the muscles in your bladder push the urine out through a tube called the urethra.

You get bladder cancer when bladder cells become abnormal and grow out of control. Over time, a tumor forms. It can spread to nearby lymph nodes and other organs. In severe cases, it can spread to distant parts of your body, including your bones, lungs, or liver.

Bladder cancer has the dubious distinction of inclusion on the top 10 list of cancers, with an estimated 81,190 new cases occurring in 2017 within the U.S. Bladder cancer is three to four times more likely to be diagnosed in men than in women and about two times higher in white men than in African-American men. Bladder cancer killed approximately 17,240 people in the U.S. in 2017. In the U.S., the bladder cancer risk for men is about one in 26 and for women about one in 90.

What is the bladder?

The urinary bladder, or the bladder, is a hollow organ in the pelvis. Most of it lies behind the pubic bone of the pelvis, but when full of urine, it can extend up into the lower part of the abdomen. Its primary function is to store urine that drains into it from the kidney through tube-like structures called the ureters. The ureters from both the kidneys open into the urinary bladder. The bladder forms a low-pressure reservoir that gradually stretches out as urine fills into it. In males, the prostate gland is located adjacent to the base of the bladder where urethra joins the bladder. From time to time, the muscular wall of the bladder contracts to expel urine through the urinary passage (urethra) into the outside world. The normal volume of the full bladder is about 400 ml-600 ml, or about 2 cups.

What are the layers of the bladder?

The bladder consists of three layers of tissue. The innermost layer of the bladder, which comes in contact with the urine stored inside the bladder, is called the "mucosa" and consists of several layers of specialized cells called "transitional cells," which are almost exclusively found in the urinary system of the body. These same cells also form the inner lining of the ureters, kidneys, and a part of the urethra. These cells form a waterproof lining within these organs to prevent the urine from going into the deeper tissue layers. These cells are also termed urothelial cells, and the mucosa is termed the urothelium.

The middle layer is a thin lining known as the 'lamina propria" and forms the boundary between the inner "mucosa" and the outer muscular layer. This layer has a network of blood vessels and nerves and is an important landmark in terms of the staging of bladder cancer (described in detail below in the bladder cancer staging section).

The outer layer of the bladder (the "muscularis") comprises of the "detrusor" muscle. This is the thickest layer of the bladder wall. Its main function is to relax slowly as the bladder fills up to provide low-pressure urine storage and then to contract to compress the bladder and expel the urine out during the act of passing urine. Outside these three layers is a variable amount of fat that lines and protects the bladder like a soft cushion and separates it from the surrounding organs such as the rectum and the muscles and bones of the pelvis.

What Is Bladder Cancer?

Bladder cancer is the unregulated growth of abnormal bladder or cancerous cells on the inner lining of the bladder wall. Most bladder cancers are detected at early stages when the tumor has not spread outside the bladder and when treatments are most successful. Bladder cancer is an uncontrolled abnormal growth and multiplication of cells in the urinary bladder, which have broken free from the normal mechanisms that keep uncontrolled cell growth in check. Invasive bladder cancer (like cancers of other organs) has the ability to spread (metastasize) to other body parts, including the lungs, bones, and liver.

Bladder cancer invariably starts from the innermost layer of the bladder (for example, the mucosa) and may invade into the deeper layers as it grows. Alternately, it may remain confined to the mucosa for a prolonged period. Visually, it may appear in various forms. Most common is a shrub-like appearance (papillary), but it may also appear

8

as a nodule, an irregular solid growth or a flat, barely perceptible thickening of the inner bladder wall (see details in subsequent sections).

What causes bladder cancer?

Bladder cancer forms when the DNA in cells in the bladder mutate or change, disabling the functions that control cell growth. In many cases, these mutated cells die or are attacked by the immune system. But some mutated cells may escape the immune system and grow out of control, forming a tumor in the bladder.

While the exact cause of bladder cancer is not known, certain risk factors are linked to the disease, including tobacco smoking and exposure to certain chemicals and gases. Also, people with a family history of bladder cancer have a high risk of developing the disease.

Symptoms of Bladder Cancer

1. Blood in Urine (Hematuria)

One sign of bladder cancer is blood in the urine, also known as hematuria. Blood in the urine does not always mean bladder cancer. Hematuria is most often caused by other conditions like trauma, infection, blood disorders, kidney problems, exercise, or certain medications. Blood in the urine may be seen by the naked eye (gross hematuria) or only detected on urine testing (microscopic hematuria). The urine may be discolored and appear brownish or darker than usual or, rarely, bright red in color.

2. Bladder Changes

Bladder cancer sometimes causes changes in bladder habits like having to urinate more often or feeling an urgent need to urinate without producing urine. Another symptom of bladder cancer is pain or burning during urination without evidence of a urinary tract infection. These symptoms of bladder problems, like bleeding, are usually caused by conditions other than cancer. In some people, bladder cancer tends to cause no symptoms until it reaches an advanced stage that is difficult to cure.

3. Smoking

Smoking is the greatest known risk factor for bladder cancer; smokers are four times more likely to get bladder cancer than nonsmokers. Harmful chemicals from cigarette smoke enter the bloodstream in the lungs and are ultimately filtered by the kidneys into the urine. This leads to a concentration of harmful chemicals inside the bladder. Experts believe that smoking causes about half of all bladder cancers in men and women.

4. Chemical Exposure

Exposure to certain chemicals on the job can increase risk of bladder cancer. Occupations that may involve exposure to cancer-causing chemicals include metal workers, hairdressers, and mechanics. Organic chemicals called aromatic amines are especially associated with bladder cancer and are used in the dye industry. Those working with dyes, metal workers, or in the manufacturing of leather, textiles, rubber, or paint should be sure to follow recommended safety protocols. Smoking increases the risk even more for these workers.

5. Urination changes

Changes in urination are more commonly a sign of a less serious condition, such as a benign tumor, infection, urinary tract infection, bladder stones, an overactive bladder or, in men, an enlarged prostate. But they also may be another early sign of bladder cancer symptoms. These changes may include:

- Frequent urination
- Pain or burning during urination
- Inability to urinate
- Feeling of urination urgency, even when the bladder isn't full
- Weak urine stream

Who is at Risk for Bladder Cancer?

Bladder cancer can affect anyone, but certain groups are at greater risk. Men are three times more likely than women to get bladder cancer. Around 90% of cases occur in people over age 55, and whites are twice as likely as African Americans to develop the condition.

Other factors that increase the risk of getting bladder cancer include a family history of the condition and previous cancer treatment. Birth defects involving the bladder increase the risk of bladder cancer. When people are born with a visible or invisible defect that connects their bladder with another organ in the abdomen, this leaves the bladder prone to frequent infection. This increases the bladder's susceptibility to cellular abnormalities that can lead to cancer. Chronic bladder inflammation (frequent bladder infections, bladder stones, and other urinary tract problems that irritate the bladder) increase the risk of developing bladder cancer.

Signs of advanced bladder cancer

When bladder tumors grow larger, or cancer cells spread to other areas of the body, they may cause symptoms including:

- Inability to urinate
- Lower back pain, generally focused on one side
- Weakness or fatigue
- Feet swelling
- Bone pain
- Pelvic pain
- Unexplained weight loss
- Appetite loss

If bladder cancer has spread, or metastasized, to another part of the body, it may cause symptoms related to that body part.

- **Lungs**: Coughing or shortness of breath
- **Liver**: Abdominal pain or jaundice (yellowing of the skin and/or eyes)
- **Bones**: Pain or fracture

If bladder cancer is suspected, your doctor may recommend tests to determine the cause of the symptoms.

What are the types of bladder cancer?

Bladder cancer is classified based on the appearance of its cells under the microscope (histological type). The type of bladder cancer has implications in selecting the appropriate treatment for the disease. For example, certain types may not respond to radiation and chemotherapy as well as others. The histological type of the cancer may also impact the extent of surgery required for maximizing the chances of cure. In addition, physicians often describe bladder cancer based on its position in the wall of the bladder. Noninvasive bladder cancers occur in the inner layer of cells (transitional cell epithelium) but do not penetrate into deeper layers. Invasive cancers penetrate into the deeper layers such as the muscle layer. Invasive cancers are more difficult to treat.

The more common types of bladder cancer are as follows:

Urothelial carcinoma (previously known as "transitional cell carcinoma") is the most common type and comprises 90%-95% of all bladder cancers. This type of cancer has two subtypes: papillary carcinoma (growing finger-like projections into the bladder lumen) and flat carcinomas that do not produce fingerlike projections. Urothelial carcinoma (transitional cell carcinoma) is strongly associated with cigarette smoking.

Adenocarcinoma of the bladder comprises about 1%-2% of all bladder cancers and is associated with prolonged inflammation and irritation. Most adenocarcinomas of the bladder are invasive.

Squamous cell carcinoma comprises 1%-2% of bladder cancers and is also associated with prolonged infection, inflammation, and irritation such as that associated with longstanding stones in the bladder. In certain parts of the Middle East and Africa (for example, Egypt), this is the predominant form of bladder cancer and is associated with chronic infection caused by Schistosoma worm (a blood fluke, that causes schistosomiasis, also termed bilharzia or snail fever).

Other rare forms of cancer found in the bladder include small cell cancer (arising in neuroendocrine cells), pheochromocytoma (rare), and sarcoma (in muscle tissue).

What foods are best when you have bladder cancer?

Many studies have explored if specific foods can fight bladder cancer. There have not been any conclusive results, but some research has shown that specific foods, especially those high in antioxidants, may have anti-cancer effects.

For now, the recommendation is to eat a healthy, well-balanced diet, which has been associated with a reduced risk of cancer recurrence and death.

A healthy eating pattern includes:

Vegetables and fruits

Vegetables and fruits provide a variety of vitamins and minerals that your body needs. Cruciferous vegetables such as broccoli, kale, and Brussels sprouts may be best because they are antioxidant-rich. Berries and citrus fruits are also good options for this reason.

Vegetables and fruits also provide fiber, which can help if you have constipation. Fiber is essential for keeping your digestive system healthy.

Protein sources

Adequate protein helps to maintain muscle mass and support your immune system. Protein sources include meat, chicken, fish, eggs, beans, lentils, soy products, nuts, seeds, and dairy. Try to include a source of protein with all meals and snacks.

Healthy fats

Fats improve the flavor and texture of food. Our body needs fat to help absorb some vitamins, produce hormones, and repair cells throughout the body. Healthy sources of fat include fish, avocados, nuts, seeds, olives, and olive oils.

Whole grains

Whole grains are grain products that have not been overly processed. This means they still contain most of their nutrients and fiber. Look for "whole grain" as the first ingredient in the ingredient list of foods you're buying.

Are there any foods or drinks to avoid?

There's a strong association between arsenic in drinking water and bladder cancer. Areas with higher levels of arsenic in the water supply have higher rates of bladder cancer. Arsenic can occur naturally in some areas or come from industry or agriculture activities.

If you use well water, make sure to have it tested at least once a year to ensure there are no problems with arsenic levels. There are treatments to remove arsenic from your water supply to make your water safe to drink.

Another area of research is the possible role of red meat in cancer risk, especially processed red meat. A 2018 meta-analysis showed a higher risk of bladder cancer in people who eat more processed red meat. Unprocessed red meat may not increase the risk of bladder cancer.

Research has also associated Western-type diets with an increased risk of bladder cancer recurrence. The Western dietary pattern is rich in highly processed foods and low in fruits and vegetables.

One 2018 study found that people who followed a Western-type diet experienced a 48 percent higher risk of bladder cancer recurrence than people who had more nutritious diets.

How do health care professionals determine bladder cancer staging?

Bladder cancer is staged using the tumor node metastases (TNM) system developed by the International Union Against Cancer (UICC) in 1997 and updated and used by the American Joint Committee on Cancer (AJCC). In addition, the American Urologic Association (ALA) has a similar staging system that varies slightly from that used by the AJCC. The combination of both staging systems appears below. This staging gives your physician a complete picture of the extent of the person's bladder cancer.

The T stage refers to the depth of penetration of the tumor from the innermost lining to the deeper layers of the bladder. The T stages are as follows:

- Tx - Primary tumor cannot be evaluated
- T0 - No primary tumor
- Ta - Noninvasive papillary carcinoma (tumor limited to the innermost lining or the epithelium)
- Tis - Carcinoma in situ (flat tumor)
- T1 - Tumor invades connective tissue under the epithelium (surface layer)
- T2 - Tumor invades muscle of the bladder

- T2a - Superficial muscle affected (inner half)
- T2b - Deep muscle affected (outer half)
- T3 - Tumor invades perivesical (around the bladder) fatty tissue
  - T3a - Microscopically (visible only on examination under the microscope)
  - T3b - Macroscopically (for example, visible tumor mass on the outer bladder tissue)
- T4 - Tumor spreads beyond fatty tissue and invades any of the following: prostate, uterus, vagina, pelvic wall, or abdominal wall

The presence and extent of involvement of the lymph nodes in the pelvic region of the body near the urinary bladder determines the N stage. The N stages are as follows:

- Nx - Regional lymph nodes cannot be evaluated
- N0 - No regional lymph node metastasis
- N1 - Metastasis in a single lymph node < 2 cm in size

- N2 - Metastasis in a single lymph node > 2 cm, but < 5 cm in size, or two or more lymph nodes < 5 cm in size

- N3 - Metastasis in a lymph node > 5 cm in size and/or to lymph nodes along the common iliac artery

The metastases or the M stage signifies the presence or absence of the spread of bladder cancer to other organs of the body.

- Mx - Distant metastasis cannot be evaluated (This stage is not used by some clinicians.)
- M0 - No distant metastasis
- M1 - Distant metastasis

A health care professional then assigns a stage:

- Stage 0a Ta N0 M0
- Stage 0is Tis N0 M0
- Stage 1 T1 N0 M0
- Stage 2 T2 N0 M0
- Stage 3 T3 N0M0

- Stage 4 T4 N0 M0, or any T, N1 or above M0 , or any T, any N, M1

The proper staging of bladder cancer is an essential step that has significant bearings on the management of this condition. The implications of bladder stage are as follows:

- It helps select proper treatment for the patient. Less aggressive treatment manages superficial disease (Ta/T1/Tis) as compared to invasive disease (T2/T3/T4).
- Invasive tumors have a higher likelihood of spread to lymph nodes and distant organs as compared to superficial tumors.
- The chances of cure and long-term survival progressively decrease as the bladder cancer stage increases.
- Staging allows proper classification of patients into groups for research studies and study of newer treatments.

What is bladder cancer grading?

A pathologist examines the tumor specimen under a microscope to determine the grading of the bladder cancer. It is a measure of the extent by which the tumor cells differ in their appearance from normal bladder cells. The greater the distortion of appearance, the higher the grade assigned. High-grade cancers are more aggressive than low-grade ones and have a greater propensity to invade into the bladder wall and spread to other parts of the body. An example of grading is as follows:

✓ **Grade 1 cancers** (or low grade or well differentiated cancers) have cells that look very much like normal cells. They tend to grow slowly and are not likely to spread.

✓ **Grade 2 cancers** have cells that look more abnormal. They are called medium grade or moderately differentiated and may grow or spread more quickly than low grade.

✓ **Grade 3 cancers** have cells that look very abnormal. They are called high grade or poorly differentiated and are more quickly growing and more likely to spread.

✓ **Grade 4 cancers** are so abnormal that they have no distinguishing features to say that they even started as bladder cells. They are undifferentiated.

Depending upon which cancer organization your clinician follows, the grades above may differ slightly. In general, they all follow the same pattern. Bladder cancers with a higher number (zero through four) are more aggressive and more difficult to treat.

In 2010, the World Health Organization and the International Society of Urologic Pathology agreed to assign the cancers grades based upon the above descriptions, shortened to G1, G2, G3, and G4.

GX is used in cases where grading cannot be assessed for technical or clinical reasons.

However, the World Health Organization (WHO) has recommended changing bladder grading to only two categories; the first category being well differentiated or low grade and the second category being poorly differentiated or high grade. The American Joint Committee on Cancer (AJCC) is adopting these categories. The older categories listed above may still be used by some clinicians and may be listed in individual patient's medical records, so they were included here.

Stage and grade of bladder cancer play a very important role not just in deciding the treatment that an individual patient should receive but also in quantifying the chances of success with that treatment. Of note, carcinoma in situ (CIS or Tis, as mentioned in the section on staging) is always high grade.

How Do Physicians Diagnose Bladder Cancer?

Like all cancers, bladder cancer is most likely to be successfully treated if detected early, when it is small and has not invaded surrounding tissues. The following measures can increase the chance of finding a bladder cancer early:

1. If you have no risk factors, pay special attention to urinary symptoms or changes in your urinary habits. If you notice symptoms that last more than a few days, see your health-care professional right away for evaluation.

2. If you have risk factors, talk to your health-care professional about screening tests, even if you have no symptoms. These tests are not performed to diagnose cancer but to look for abnormalities that suggest an

early cancer. If these tests find abnormalities, they should be followed by other, more specific tests for bladder cancer.

3. **Screening tests:** Screening tests are usually performed periodically, for example, once a year or once every five years. The most widely used screening tests are medical interview, history, physical examination, urinalysis, urine cytology, and cystoscopy.

4. **Medical interview:** Your health-care professional will ask you many questions about your medical condition (past and present), medications, work history, and habits and lifestyle. From this, he or she will develop an idea of your risk for bladder cancer.

5. **Physical examination:** Your health-care professional may insert a gloved finger into your vagina, rectum, or

both to feel for any lumps that might indicate a tumor or another cause of bleeding.

6. **Urinalysis:** This test is actually a collection of tests for abnormalities in the urine such as blood, protein, and sugar (glucose). Any abnormal findings should be investigated with more definitive tests. Blood in the urine, hematuria, although more commonly associated with noncancerous (benign) conditions, may be associated with bladder cancer and thus deserves further evaluation.

7. **Urine cytology:** The cells that make up the inner bladder lining regularly slough off and are suspended in the urine and excreted from the body during urination. In this test, a sample of the urine is examined under a microscope to look for abnormal cells that might suggest cancer.

8. **Cystoscopy:** This is a type of endoscopy. A very narrow tube with a light and a camera on the end (cystoscope) is used to examine the inside of the bladder to look for abnormalities such as tumors. The cystoscope is inserted into the bladder through the urethra. The camera transmits pictures to a video monitor, allowing direct viewing of the inside of the bladder wall.

9. **Fluorescence cystoscopy** (blue light cystoscopy) is a special type of cystoscopy involving the placement of a light-activated drug into the bladder, which is picked up by the cancer cells. The cancer cells are identified by shining a blue light through the cystoscope and looking for fluorescent cells (the cells that have picked up the drug).

These tests are also used to diagnose bladder cancers in people who are having symptoms. The following tests might be done if bladder cancer is suspected:

1. **CT scan:** This is similar to an X-ray film but shows much greater detail. It gives a three-dimensional view of your bladder, the rest of your urinary tract (especially the kidneys), and your pelvis to look for masses and other abnormalities.

2. **Retrograde pyelogram:** This study involves injecting dye into the ureter, the tube that connects the kidney to the bladder, to fill the ureter and inside of the kidney. The dye is injected by placing a small hollow tube through the cystoscope and inserting the hollow tube into the opening of the ureter in the bladder. X-ray pictures are taken during filling of the ureter and kidney to look for areas that don't fill out with the dye, known as filling defects, which could be tumors involving the ureter and/or lining of the kidney. This test may be performed to evaluate the kidneys and ureters in individuals who are allergic to intravenous

dye and thus cannot have a CT scan with contrast (dye) performed.

3. **MRI (magnetic resonance imaging)** is also an alternative test to look at the kidneys, ureters, and bladder in individuals with contrast (dye) allergies.

4. **Biopsy:** Tiny samples of your bladder wall are removed, usually during cystoscopy. The samples are examined by a physician who specializes in diagnosing diseases by looking at tissues and cells (pathologist). Small tumors are sometimes completely removed during the biopsy process. (transurethral resection of bladder tumor [TURBT]).

5. **Urine tests:** Other urine tests may be performed to rule out conditions or to obtain specifics about urine abnormalities. For example, a urine culture may be

done to rule out an infection. The presence of certain antibodies and other markers may indicate cancer. Some of these tests may be helpful in detecting recurrent cancer very early.

6. **Urine tumor markers:** There are several newer molecular tests that look at substances in the urine that might help determine if a bladder cancer is present. These include UroVysion (FISH), BTA tests, ImmunoCyt, NMP 22 BladderChek, and BladderCx.

If a tumor is found in the bladder, other tests may be performed, either at the time of diagnosis or later, to determine whether the cancer has spread to other parts of the body.

7. **Ultrasound:** This is similar to the technique used to look at a fetus in a pregnant woman's uterus. In this

painless test, a handheld device run over the surface of the skin uses sound waves to examine the contours of the bladder and other structures in the pelvis. This can show the size of a tumor and may show if it has spread to other organs.

8. **Chest X-ray film:** A simple X-ray film of the chest can sometimes show whether bladder cancer has spread to the lungs.

9. **CT scan:** This technique is used to detect metastatic disease in the lungs, liver, abdomen, or pelvis, as well as to evaluate whether obstruction of the kidneys has occurred. PET/CT, a special type of CT scan, may be helpful in the evaluation of individuals with invasive, higher-stage bladder cancer to determine if the bladder cancer has spread.

10. **MRI (magnetic resonance imaging)** may also be useful in the staging of bladder cancer and can be performed without contrast in individuals with a contraindication to contrast.

11. **Bone scan:** This test involves having a tiny amount of a radioactive substance injected into your veins. A full body scan will show any areas where the cancer may have affected the bones.

Bladder Cancer Treatment: Surgery

Transurethral Resection

Early-stage cancers are most commonly treated by transurethral surgery. An instrument (resectoscope) with a small wire loop is inserted through the urethra and into the bladder. The loop removes a tumor by cutting or burning it with electrical current, allowing it to be extracted from the bladder.

Partial and Radical Cystectomy

Partial cystectomy includes the removal of part of the bladder. This operation is usually for low-grade tumors that have invaded the bladder wall but are limited to a small area of the bladder. In a radical cystectomy, the entire bladder is removed, as well as its surrounding lymph nodes and other areas that contain cancerous cells. If the cancer has metastasized outside of the bladder and into neighboring tissue, other organs may also be removed such as the uterus and ovaries in women and the prostate in men.

The use of a bladder catheter is common among bladder cancer patients.

Bladder Cancer Treatment: Urinary Diversion After Surgery

When the entire bladder is removed the surgeon will create an alternate way for urine to be stored and passed. This procedure is called urinary diversion. Depending on preference, a bag can either be placed inside or outside of the body to collect urine. Non-continent urinary diversion is when a urostomy bag is placed outside the body, worn under the clothes. Continent urinary diversion consists of a pouch, made from intestinal tissue, inside the body to hold urine. In a newly introduced surgical procedure, the insertion of an artificial bladder has also been successful for some patients.

Intravenous therapy used for chemotherapy treating bladder cancer.

Bladder Cancer Treatment: Chemotherapy

Chemotherapy is given in some cases before surgery to shrink bladder cancer tumors. It can also be used after surgery to destroy any remaining tumor cells. Chemotherapy may be given intravenously or administered directly into the bladder (intravesical chemotherapy). Intravesical chemotherapy is effective in decreasing the recurrence rate of superficial bladder cancers on a short-term basis, but not effective against bladder cancer that has already invaded the muscular walls. Systemic or intravenous chemotherapy is required when the cancer has deeply penetrated the bladder, lymph nodes, or other organs.

Chemotherapy Side Effects

Side effects vary from patient to patient. Common side effects of systemic chemotherapy include the following:

41

- Nausea and vomiting
- Loss of appetite
- Hair loss
- Sores on the inside of the mouth or in the digestive tract
- Feeling tired or lacking energy
- Increased susceptibility to infection
- Easy bruising or bleeding
- Numbness or tingling in the hands or feet

Bladder Cancer Treatment: Immunotherapy

Immunotherapy involves the administration of helpful bacteria through a catheter into the bladder to trigger the immune system to attack both the bacteria and the cancer cells. Immunotherapy is only given in stages Ta, T1, and CIS (carcinoma in situ) bladder cancers. Bacillus Calmette-Guerin (BCG) is a type of bacteria used in this therapy. Intravesical BCG treatment is given once a week and can be used after surgery to lower the chance of tumor recurrence. Immunotherapy side effects can include irritation of the bladder, minor bleeding in the b adder, and flu-like symptoms.

Bladder Cancer Treatment: Radiation

What is Radiation?

Radiation therapy is the use of painless, invisible, high-energy radiation that can kill both healthy and cancerous cells. Radiation can be used as an alternative apprcach or in addition to chemotherapy or surgery to destroy cancer cells.

External Radiation

External radiation is produced by a machine outside the body. The machine aims a concentrated beam of radiation at the tumor. External radiation is typically given five days a week for five to seven weeks.

Internal Radiation

Internal radiation consists of inserting a small pellet of radioactive material inside the bladder. The treatment lasts several days and patients are required to stay in the hospital until the pellet is removed.

Radiation Side Effects

Radiation therapy also has side effects, which can include fatigue, nausea, skin irritation, pain with urination, and diarrhea.

There are no alternative treatments to cure bladder cancer.

Alternative Treatments for Bladder Cancer

There are no alternative or complementary therapies that have been shown to prevent or cure bladder cancer. Ongoing research studies are examining the role of green tea or broccoli sprouts as potential complementary treatments. Consult your doctor before starting any such "therapies".

Bladder Cancer Survival Rates

As with most cancers, survival rates are dependent upon the stage or extent of spread of the cancer when it is found. About 50% of bladder cancers are detected when the tumor is limited to the inner lining of the bladder, and 5-year survival rates for this early stage of cancer are nearly 100%. Cancers that have spread further typically have lower survival rates. Today the relative survival rates for all stages of bladder cancer are 77% at 5 years, 70% at 10 years, and 65% at 15 years.

Changes for Men

Some men may have trouble getting an erection, but in younger men, this may improve over time. Semen cannot be produced if the surgery involved removal of the prostate gland and seminal vesicles.

Changes for Women

In women, the uterus, ovaries, and part of the vagina are removed during radical cystectomy. This permanently stops menstruation and prohibits all future pregnancies. Women who undergo surgery for bladder cancer may also find that sex is less comfortable, and achieving orgasms may be difficult.

When Is Follow-up Needed After Bladder Cancer Treatment?

After you complete your treatment, you will undergo a series of tests to determine how well your treatment worked at getting rid of your cancer.

- If the results show remaining cancer, your urologic oncologist will recommend further treatment.
- If the results show no remaining cancer, he or she will recommend a schedule for follow-up visits. These visits will include tests to see whether the cancer has come back. They will be frequent at first because of the risk of the cancer recurrence after treatment.
- If you still have your native bladder, follow-up will include interval cystoscopy and urine tests.
- If you have undergone radical cystectomy, follow-up will include imaging tests of your chest and abdomen.

Bladder Cancer Prevention

The best way to prevent bladder cancer is to avoid exposure to agents that cause the disease. People who don't smoke are three to four times less likely to get bladder cancer as compared to smokers. Continuing to smoke after the diagnosis of bladder cancer portends a poorer outcome and increases the chance of the disease coming back after treatment. Avoidance of occupational exposure to cancer-causing chemicals such as aniline dyes may also be important. Despite research in this area no medication or dietary supplement has been conclusively demonstrated to decrease the risk of bladder cancer in normal individuals. However, recent studies of patients taking atorvastatin (Lipitor) to lower cholesterol have suggested the drug may lower the risk of prostatic cancer and by inference, bladder cancer, but this needs further study.

It is always advisable to follow a healthy lifestyle. Stop smoking and limit alcohol consumption to 1 to 2 drinks a day. A healthy diet contains lots of fruits, vegetables, whole grains, and correct portion sizes of lean meats. Regular exercise and having checkups can also help you support your health and provide peace of mind. Avoid unsafe chemical exposures and keep protected if working with chemicals.

New and Experimental Treatments for Bladder Cancer

New treatments are being investigated for bladder cancer. These include photodynamic therapy, gene therapy, and targeted therapy. Clinical trials are available to test some of these or other new therapies.

Photodynamic Therapy

Photodynamic therapy uses a laser light and chemicals to kills cancer cells and shrink tumors. A few days before treatment, the patient is given light-sensitive compounds intravenously that sensitizes cancer cells to the light rays emitted by a laser. A small scope with a laser is then introduced into the bladder through the urethra and is aimed at the tumor.

Gene Therapy

Gene therapy refers to the introduction of cells with laboratory-altered DNA into the body in order to prevent the mutation and spread of cancerous cells or to attack cancerous cells and tumors by cutting off blood supply or causing internal cellular death to targeted cancer cells. Gene therapy often requires the use of a patient's blood or bone marrow may in order to perform the procedure. Experimental in nature, gene therapy is a newly emerging procedure with a growing research base. Some scientists believe gene therapy may be the best way to find a cure for cancer.

Targeted Therapy

Targeted therapies are directed at limiting growth of cancer cells. Targeted therapy uses drugs to interfere with specific molecules involved in carcinogenesis and tumor growth.

Risk factors for bladder cancer

General

Gender: Men are at a higher risk than women of getting bladder cancer. According to the American Cancer Society, men have an approximately 1 in 26 chance of developing bladder cancer in their lifetime. For women, this chance is about 1 in 86.

✓ **Age:** Most people who get bladder cancer are older in age. The average age at diagnosis is 73, and 90 percent of patients are over age 55.

✓ **Race:** Bladder cancer is twice as common among Caucasians as African Americans. This disease is less common among Hispanics, Asians and Native Americans.

Genetics

Family history: Individuals with a family member who has or has had bladder cancer are at an increased risk for developing this disease. Sometimes, family members with bladder cancer have been exposed to the same carcinogen. Other times, they may all have certain genetic abnormalities associated with bladder cancer. Specifically, mutations in genes known as GNT and NAT may trigger changes in the body's breakdown of some toxins, which may in turn cause cancer cells to form in the bladder wall.

Other inherited genetic syndromes are also ccnsidered bladder cancer risk factors, such as:

✓ **Rb1:** An altered form of Rb1, retinoblastoma gene, is associated with cancer of the eye in infants, and may increase your bladder cancer risks.

✓ **Cowden disease:** This syndrome, linked to an abnormal form of the gene PTEN, may trigger breast cancer and thyroid cancer, and increases the risk of bladder cancer.

✓ **Lynch syndrome:** This genetic condition, also known as hereditary non-polyposis colorectal cancer, is usually tied to colon and endometrial cancer. However, this syndrome may also increase the risk of bladder cancer and cancer of the ureter.

Recipe and nutrition tips

There are no recipes specifically for people with bladder cancer. In general, it's best to eat a variety of healthy foods. However, if you're concerned you might not be getting enough nutrients, here are some tips for getting more from your diet:

Add more vegetables

You can add extra vegetables into casseroles, soups, and stews. Frozen vegetables can be helpful. They're just as healthy as fresh vegetables and you don't have to do extra washing and cutting before using them.

Add healthy fats

Consider using olive oil in dressings or drizzling it on or into other foods. Spreading nut butters or avocado on toast or crackers is another possible option.

Add protein

When you have cancer, your body needs more protein. Adding a source of protein to meals and snacks can help you meet your daily needs. Whole eggs, fish, nuts, seeds, and Greek yogurt are just a few examples of healthy protein sources.

You can easily add skim milk powder to anything milk-based to boost the protein content. You can also try adding canned beans or lentils into stews or soups or shredded cheese to eggs, potatoes, or cooked vegetables.

What if eating is difficult?

There are many reasons why it might be hard to get the nutrients you need, especially if you have loss of appetite from cancer treatments, according to the American Cancer

Society. If you're feeling fatigued or nauseous, eating can be challenging.

Here are some tips that might help:

- ✓ Accept help from family or friends who offer to buy groceries or bring you meals or snacks.
- ✓ Keep simple snacks and meals in your home to minimize prep time.
- ✓ Do your best to eat something every 2 to 3 hours.
- ✓ Eat in a relaxing, pleasant environment.
- ✓ Avoid filling up on fluids before meals.
- ✓ You may find bland, starchy foods such as pasta, crackers, toast, or cereal easier to tolerate.
- ✓ If you're having trouble eating enough, focus on high-calorie, high-protein foods like eggs, peanut butter, and cheese to increase your calorie consumption.
- ✓ Consider using nutritional supplement shakes or making smoothies if drinking feels easier than eating something more solid.

✓ For some people, sniffing fresh lemon or using ginger tea or sucking on ginger candies can help.

How Common Is Bladder Cancer Recurrence?

The number of people with bladder cancer varies dramatically depending on the stage of the cancer at the time of diagnosis.

Nearly 90% of people treated for superficial bladder cancer (Ta, T1, CIS) survive for at least five years after treatment.

The average survival time for patients with metastatic bladder cancer spread to other organs is 12 to 18 months. Some live longer than that, and some less time than that. Historically it has been noted that most patients that respond to treatment live longer than those who co not.

Recurrent cancer indicates a more aggressive type and a poor outlook for long-term survival for patients with advanced stage bladder cancer. Recurrent low-grade superficial bladder cancer is rarely life-threatening unless it is neglected such as if a patient does not bring recurrent symptoms or problems to the doctor's attention and it becomes invasive bladder cancer.

Conclusion

The 5-year survival rate for bladder cancer is about 77%. That means that about 7 out of 10 people who are diagnosed with the disease will still be alive 5 years later. But that's just an estimate. Your outcome is based on your unique situation. That includes things like your age, overall health, how early the cancer was found, and how well it responds to treatment.

Most bladder cancers are of a type called transitional cell because they affect the same kinds of cells (transitional cells) that are usually the cancerous cells responsible for cancers of the renal pelvis and ureters.

Bladder cancer most often causes blood in the urine.

To make the diagnosis, doctors insert a thin, flex ble tube with a camera (cystoscope) through the urethra into the bladder.

Many cancers are treated with removal, using a cystoscope (for surface cancers) or by removing the bladder (for deeper cancers).

About 83,730 new cases of bladder cancer are diagnosed every year in the United States. According to 2021 estimates, more than 17,200 people die of bladder cancer every year. About 3 times as many men as women develop bladder cancer.

Smoking is the greatest single risk factor and seems to be one of the causes in at least half of all new cases. Certain chemicals that are used in industry can become concentrated in the urine and cause cancer, although exposure to these chemicals is decreasing. These chemicals include hydrocarbons, aniline dyes (such as naphthylamine used in the dye industry) and chemicals used in the rubber, electric, cable, paint, and textile industries. Long-term exposure to some drugs, especially cyclophosphamide, increases the risk of bladder cancer. The chronic irritation that occurs with a parasitic infection called schistosomiasis or with bladder stones, urinary tract infections, or chronic catheter use also predisposes people to bladder cancer, although irritation accounts for only a small number of all cases.

It is not possible for a doctor to predict the exact course of a disease as it will depend on the person's individual circumstances. However, your doctor may give you a prognosis, the likely outcome of your disease, based on the type of cancer you have, your test results, the rate of tumour growth, as well as your age, fitness and medical history.

Bladder cancer can be effectively treated if it is found early, before it spreads outside the bladder

Made in the USA
Las Vegas, NV
03 August 2023

75612102R00036